ABANDONED ARKANSAS

EAKER AIR FORCE BASE

GAGE FEARS

America Through Time is an imprint of Fonthill Media LLC
www.through-time.com
office@through-time.com

Published by Arcadia Publishing by arrangement with Fonthill Media LLC
For all general information, please contact Arcadia Publishing:
Telephone: 843-853-2070
Fax: 843-853-0044
E-mail: sales@arcadiapublishing.com
For customer service and orders:
Toll-Free 1-888-313-2665

www.arcadiapublishing.com

First published 2023

ISBN 978-1-63499-468-2

Typeset in Trade Gothic 10pt on 15pt
Printed and bound in England

"A B-52 with a full nuclear payload, is the seventh most powerful country in the world."

CONTENTS

ABOUT THE AUTHOR

GAGE FEARS started writing at an early age, alongside multiple forms of art. After publishing photos of an abandoned radio station in Arkansas, he was noticed by Abandoned Arkansas. And the rest is history. Gage is a member of three historical societies, ordained minister, TWIC card holder, multi-instrumentalist, and military fanatic/historian. He is a contributor to the National Cold War Center; the Jacksonville Museum of Military History in Jacksonville, Arkansas; and the Rock and Roll Highway 67 Museum in Newport, Arkansas. Gage is a historical preservationist, just like his grandmother.

INTRODUCTION

E aker Air Force Base is located three miles northwest of Blytheville, Arkansas. Of the 3,771 acres the base is composed of, two-thirds of the land is abandoned. Currently, the main tarmac is used as Blytheville's airport. In its prime, it housed over 3,000 service members, and a whole fleet of Strategic Air Command B-52 "BUFF" Stratofortresses. Eaker Air Force Base was complete with swimming pools, tennis courts, a grocery store, a dental office, a nine-hole golf course, a theater, multiple clubs, visitation centers, a gym, and on-base housing for military families.

Today the base is mostly in a decrepit state of disrepair, though local organizations and legal entities constantly fight to preserve the base. The majority of the base's housing is still in use, a few buildings are in use, and the tarmac is now the Arkansas Aeroplex. At the height of the Cold War, Eaker Air Force Base was home to the 97th Bombardment Wing, the 42nd Air Division, the 97th Air Refueling Squadron, the 97th Supply Squadron, the 97th Organizational Maintenance Squadron, the 820th Medical Group, and many more. All of these were under the Strategic Air Command.

Blytheville was built with a runway that stretched to the length of over 11,000 feet. The alert pad was positioned at the Southeast end of the runway, while the apron and "blast walls," as well as the main tower, were on the west side of the runway.

The control tower, pre-1988

1

WHAT'S IN A NAME?

Eaker Air Force Base was originally named Blytheville Army Airfield when it was built in 1942. In 1953, under new command of the newly established United States Air Force, the base was reopened as Blytheville Air Force Base. In 1988, the base was renamed to honor World War II General Ira C. Eaker. Nowadays, the base goes by a few names. Eaker Air Force Base Historic District, Arkansas International Airport, and Blytheville Municipal Airport. Though it is referred to as these names, the airport officially goes by Arkansas Aeroplex. Eaker was on the base closure list in the late '80s, and the common belief is that naming Blytheville to Eaker Air Force Base would save it from closure. This only helped for about five years.

Pre-1988 sign at entrance

2

GENERAL IRA C. EAKER

General Ira C. Eaker was born in Field Creek, Texas, in 1896. His career started off in the 64th Infantry as a second lieutenant in the U.S. Army's Officer Reserves. In 1917, he would become a second lieutenant in the Regular Army. In 1918, he detached from the 64th Infantry and went to Texas to receive flying instruction.

In 1920, he returned to the U.S. from Fort Mills. In 1924, Ira C. Eaker was named executive assistant in the Office of Air Service. Ira would go on for many years

General Ira Eaker

after climbing the ranks, earning many titles, and leading many campaigns as a pilot and commander. Ira C. Eaker recorded over 12,000 flying hours in a span of thirty years. He retired in 1947 as deputy commander of the Army Air Forces and chief of the Air Staff. Ira was a Congressional Gold Medal awardee, a highly decorated general (four stars to be exact), and had a long list of foreign awards from his service. Ira was buried with full military honors at Arlington National Cemetery in 1987. In 1988, Blytheville Air Force Base changed to Eaker Air Force Base to honor the general.

3

BLYTHEVILLE ARMY AIRFIELD

During World War II, the United States needed more areas to train pilots and launch aircraft to respond to the threat on the Eastern Front. Arkansas had six Army airfields: Blytheville, Walnut Ridge, Grider, Newport, Stuttgart, and Adams Field. Blytheville was the only advanced training base in Arkansas.

When the base was founded in 1942, the headquarters was a single-story farmhouse. The Army Air Force had a sawmill running around the clock 24/7 to create lumber for the construction of the base.

Blytheville was the only two-engine training base in Arkansas. Under the command of the 326th Base Headquarters and Air Base Squadron, pilots would train in aircraft such as the Beechcraft AT-10, and Curtiss-Wright AT-9s.

In 1943, the construction of Blytheville Army Airfield was completed, and training immediately started.

Blytheville became the only major Army Airfield in Arkansas (aside from Little Rock) to stay in military use after World War II. Most either were abandoned, returned to farmland, or became municipal airports such as Grider and Walnut Ridge. During its years as an Army Airfield, Blytheville was assigned four auxiliary airfields. The airfields were located in Manila, Arkansas, Cooter, Hornersville, and Steele, Missouri.

The 809th Army Air Forces Base Unit was assigned to the base and the mission was to serve as a training ground for C-46 and C-47 aircraft, as well as Waco CG-4A gliders. The unit was under control of the I Troop Carrier Command. That same year, the training facility was closed due to the closing of World War II.

In the spring of 1946, after over half a year of silence, the Tactical Air Command assumed control of the airfield. Its mission changed to become a "processing center" for those being discharged from the Army Air Forces after the end of World War II. Later that year, by ruling of the War Assets Administration, the United States government was to sell off surplus assets and property to the general public.

Flying over the USAAF barracks

World War II twin-engined trainer aircraft at Blytheville Army Airfield

4

THE WASPS

The WASP program tasked select women with many key roles on airfields across the nation. Blytheville had their own team. Airwomen were tasked with testing electronics of aircraft, testing aircraft by means of flights, and ferrying aircraft.

The program was composed of just over 1,100 women, though the program and its members were not considered truly military nor pilots until the 1970s. In 1942, at the graduation ceremony, it was believed that women could not fly as well as men. The commanding general of the U.S. Army Air Forces, Henry Arnold, went as far as saying that he doubted a woman could control a B-17. However, two years later they proved him and everyone else wrong. These women had proved themselves capable of flying aircraft such as the B-25 and the B-29.

Patricia Kenworthy was one key airwoman of the program. After her military service, she was a field hockey player in the All-America team and a player for the United States' national team in Europe. In 1988, Kenworthy was inducted into the U.S. Field Hockey Hall of Fame. During her service, she claimed to be 5'2". In a Stearman, she was known to sit on three pillows. In 2010, Kenworthy, and approximately 200 other WASP members were awarded the Congressional Gold Medal for their service.

Above: WASP team

Left: Blytheville WASP airwoman, Patricia Kenworth

5

BOEING B-52 STRATOFORTRESS

Since 1955, the B-52 Stratofortress has been America's go-to long-distance strategic bomber. Since then, there have been only 744 aircraft built by Boeing. The last model 61-0040, was produced in 1962. It was rolled out of Boeing's Wichita plant. The B-52 Stratofortress was the answer to all the problems found in the Convair B-36 Peacemaker and the B-24. In the late 1940s, the Strategic Air Command had testified for the need for new long-range bombers. At that time, the U.S. Navy had been doing the same for a "supercarrier." The U.S. Air Force had procured the funds. Though, the result was what was to become known as the "billion-dollar blunder." The B-36 was too heavy and couldn't hold the desired amount of payload. In fact, at one point, the Strategic Air Command had replaced one of the fuel cells of the B-36 to carry more payload.

Even though the Air Force needed a long-range bomber to go farther with fewer pit stops, the B-36 proved to be a nightmare. The B-36 was grossly inefficient and slow with its six prop motors. Due to such problems, the U.S. Air Force needed to look at the long-range bombing in a different way. The B-36 never saw any form of combat.

The B-52 Stratofortress had solved every issue the Air Force ran into with earlier bombers. The Air Force needed a long-distance bomber that could travel all the way to the former U.S.S.R., drop a payload on a target, and travel back without needing refueling. The bomber had improved range. It was also able to land without needing its aft landing gear down to create drag. Boeing transitioned from a tandem cockpit (like the B-47 Stratojet that preceded the B-52) design to a traditional "side-by-side" cockpit. Boeing did keep the tandem landing gear design from the B-47 to help with the bomber's aerodynamics and to prevent having to deal with a trim change after dropping a payload. The B-47 was a high-level bomber that dropped free-fall nuclear bombs. Once the invention of surface to air missiles came along, it was obsolete with its slow-revving engines, outdated radar technology, and 20-millimeter guns.

Since the prototype was first built in 1948, there have been eight versions/upgrades. The B-52A and B-52B were test models. The bomber shared many designs and technology with the B-47 Stratojet. Originally, the B-52 Stratofortress had a wooden vertical rudder/stabilizer setup. The plane also had dry wings until the invention of the wet wing came along. (A wet wing is a wing that is sealed and used as a fuel tank.) This increased stability in low-altitude situations.

Until the G variation was built, the tail gunner had to "jettison" the gun to bail out. Once the G variation came along, the tail gun was controlled from upfront. When the G and H models came about, clamps holding the fuel tanks in a place plagued the aircraft with constant leaking issues. In the seventy-plus years the aircraft has been in service, it has acquired numerous upgrades. In 2006, the B-52 became the first-ever aircraft to use alternative fuel. The original models were built with Pratt & Whitney J57-P-1W turbojets. C, D, and E variants were built with an updated version of the previously mentioned engine.

In 1996, Rolls-Royce and Boeing collaborated and proposed a re-engine program to the U.S. Air Force. The new engine proposed was the Rolls-Royce RB211-535 engine. In 1997, the Air Force declined the program. In 2020, however, the Air Force had started a program in partnership with the two companies to re-engine the aircraft. The new engine proposed is the Rolls-Royce F130. The Air Force purchased over 600 engines at a cost of over two billion dollars.

ALERT! ALERT! ALERT!

Barksdale AFB B52 performing A.C.E. training at Blytheville, January 2022

Pre-1980s photo of a B-52 in front of the control tower (note the camo on top, flash white on bottom paint job)

6

A BIRD WITHOUT A TAIL

On January 10, 1964, a B-52H loaned to Boeing by the USAF was testing the structural integrity of, and new technology for, the aircraft. The aircraft in question was tail number 61-0023. During its test flight, Boeing was performing tests to show the aircraft's resilience against low-altitude turbulence. A strong gust of wind has pushed the aft section of the aircraft to the left then to the right. Unbeknownst to the crew, over 70 percent of the vertical stabilizer and rudder assembly had been sheared off. The crew started to lose control of the plane and began a bail-out procedure. Before the first man could bail out, the pilot had realized they had marginal control over the aircraft.

The aircraft was set on course to Boeing's headquarters in Wichita, Kansas. However, due to high traffic in that area, the aircraft had to change its course and headed for Blytheville Air Force Base instead. The crew lowered its speed to 30 knots above the minimum cruising speed of the aircraft. They lowered all its aft landing gear and transferred the fuel towards the bow of the aircraft. This ensured a stabilization of the aircraft. Serial Number 61-0023 landed safely in Blytheville. Charles Fisher would forever be known as "Mr. B-52" for his quick thinking, response to a crisis, and heroic duties.

61-0023 was grounded at Blytheville for repairs. It was stored in a hangar on the south end of the ramp. The bomber's aft fuselage was tweaked by the impact of the wind.

Without a tail, rerouting to Blytheville

Charles and the crew that bravely manned the B-52 to Blytheville without a tail

7

BOEING KC-135 STRATOTANKER

The KC-135 Stratotanker, as most other noteworthy aircraft, was born out of necessity. The U.S. Air Force needed a long-range aircraft able to refuel others. The KC-135 replaced the KC-97, as the latter could not keep up with the advancements of aircraft technology, and the increasing speeds of such. A total of 820 KC-135s have been produced since 1956. 732 of the aircraft were specifically aerial tankers. Eighty-eight of the aircraft built were modified versions to serve specific purposes such as reconnaissance aircraft and cargo carriers.

The KC-135, along with the B-52, is one of the only fixed-wing aircraft with over fifty years of service. It has been renowned as the U.S.A.F.'s main aerial fueling aircraft. These aircraft share a similar design to the Boeing 707. It can carry up to eighty passengers and 202,000 pounds of fuel. This is made possible by four CFM International F108-CF-100 turbofans (on the current variation). These create 21,600 pounds of thrust each.

KC-135s fuel other aircraft through an extendable boom on the aft section. The boom is controlled by an operator lying prone under the cargo deck of the aircraft. Compared to hose-style fueling systems, flying booms of KC-135s are very unforgiving to errors.

The tanker was designed for "optimum maintenance under field condition." This means almost everything and anything is accessible by some type of door or latch, from radar to throttle cables. It is planned to be in service until 2040, but due to maintenance costs, a replacement is in the works. Just as Pratt & Whitney cannot reproduce parts for the engines of the B-52 due to technology and cost issues, Boeing cannot reproduce parts for the KC-135.

The current replacement for the KC-135 is the Boeing KC-46 Pegasus. It is powered by two Pratt & Whitney PW4062 high-bypass turbofan engines. These create over 62,000 pounds of thrust. It can carry up to 212,000 pounds of fuel. The KC-46 is designed off of the Boeing 767 platform. The KC46 uses a modernized KC-10 fuel boom.

The U.S. Air Force plans on having 197 KC-46s in their ever-growing fleet by 2027.

KC-135

KC-135 being loaded with cargo

N.C.O. Club bathroom

BLYTHEVILLE
ARKANSAS

U.S. AIR FORCE
0231

COMMISSARY

MMS MUNITIONS CONTROL

8

THE STRATEGIC AIR COMMAND

Eaker Air Force Base was under control of the Strategic Air Command, a United States Air Force Major Command (or MAJCOM). The Strategic Air Command's duty was to be the first line of defense against major enemies and be a major nuclear deterrent. The Strategic Air Command was responsible for the nation's nuclear arsenal, operating the Department of Defense's Information grid, and the nation's "strategic deterrence." One large part of the Strategic Air Command's duties was a global strike initiative.

Born from the Army Air Force, the Strategic Air command was composed of General Spaatz's European command, the Strategic Air Forces, the Twentieth, Fifteenth, and Eighth Air Forces. During the Cold War, the S.A.C. had all its bases under an eagle's eye, especially every person on or around their bases. During the "alert days," while on the apron, there was a system in place to ensure security.

With the S.A.C., security was very important. This system was known as the "Two-Person Concept" or Air Force Instruction (AFI) 91-104. It was designed to prevent unauthorized/incorrect handling and procedure of a nuclear weapon, weapons system, or critical component. At all times, especially if a bomber was loaded with nuclear weapons, this system enforced that two airmen had to be in eye sight of each other. If the two had failed to do so, security would have said airmen apprehended and detained. The Two-Person Concept is still in effect as of today. This instruction went on par with the concept of the "No-Lone Zone."

Blytheville, like every S.A.C. base, had a "No-Lone Zone." The zone is marked clearly with bold red lines on the apron. Guards with M16 rifles stood at numerous spots around the alert pad. It did not matter if it was raining. These guards were part of the 97th Security Police Squadron. On the alert pad, across from building 1225, is the Alert Fire Team Facility, or building 1218. The No-Lone Zone also had sensors that were buried in the concrete along the bold, red lines that detected if someone had crossed the line. These sensors were so sensitive that even small animals would constantly trip the alarm. "S.P.s" would stand at each bomber for eight-and-a-half hours at a time on guard with a two-channel Motorola radio and a M16 rifle.

Building 1218 housed an emergency response team known for its "fifteen troops in five minutes" team. This facility housed its own ammunition room and a rack for M16 rifles. It had portholes on every wall facing outwards in every direction. In case of the need to defend the alert pad, the 97th S.P.S. would insert the barrel of their rifle into the porthole and fire outwards. Currently, it is empty, though it is to be restored and set up as an exhibit for the National Cold War Center. 1218 also housed an armored vehicle with a turret and a mounted M60 machine gun. This vehicle was affectionately nicknamed the "Peacekeeper." They were powered by a Mopar 360 c.i. (and later the 318 c.i.) V8, and had foam filled tires. The Peacekeeper was constantly prone to overheating and vapor locking and had a terrible issue with tipping. The foam-filled tires usually went flat due to little to no use.

The Strategic Air Command enforced a sense and standard of urgency. Random "exercises" would always take place at any given time, at any given location. This was part of the "Global Shield" program. S.A.C. would test the various chains of command as well as the performance and maintenance of bases, units, and airmen. These exercises would never be disclosed to anyone on base. This would be to prevent preparation as one can never prepare for an immediate, full-scale nuclear attack.

When these exercises occurred, a false crisis would be created for the situation. Most of the time, the crisis would be a nuclear attack on United States bases and key "targets" the D.O.D. knew Russia had their eyes on. Certain bases would be sent on alert and perform their response as diligently, efficiently, and as fast as they could. Multiple birds would be sent in the air: several spy aircraft, tankers, bombers, and even an airborne command and control center known as "Operation Looking Glass." The exercises would occur more often than any actual crisis ever did. Global Shield exercises varied in intensity of DEFCON levels.

The exercises saw the involvement of the President, his entire cabinet, the top commanders of the D.O.D., as well as the S.A.C. Once a crisis was imminent, the President would be put onto either Air Force One, or into a secure bunker, or onto Operation Looking Glass (the rarest situation of them all). The Commander-in-Chief of the S.A.C. would be alerted and then given a very short amount of time to delegate a response. Most of the time he would end up on Operation Looking Glass.

The responding bases involved in the exercises would enact a nuclear alert protocol. In an alert situation, aircraft would perform M.I.T.O. (Minimum Interval Take Off) scrambles. Any and all responding aircrew would rush to the alert pad and jump start the aircraft. Once on the runway, the aircraft were run wide open to

Strategic Air Command logo on a
B-58 Hustler on display at Little Rock
Air Force Base

Always on watch, 24/7

get off the ground quickly. This was usually referred to as "running dirty," as B-52s are known to create giant clouds of burnt fuel.

Once all alert aircraft are off the ground, emergency response teams would be dispatched to the responding bases. Teams would deactivate lights, radar houses, and satellite equipment on the ground. This would be part of a situation where a specific base would be attacked. Responding aircraft would have to react and decide on a return plan. At the end of Global Shield exercises, units would be scored on their overall performance.

Home of the 42nd Air Division and the 97th Bombardment Wing

```
RCV MSG #    TIME    RADAY                    RET MSG #      'ROUTINE'
  03079     2321    128/89                      10329

AC (BW/CC) CMS (DO) DOC DON DOT DOX DOJ DOB IN LGC LGS LGT LGX OPR____J2_
MA PA RM SE SG CSG/CC IM DE MS DPC JA SI SP SS SV OSI SPVR______
ARS ACEDET BX FC SACMET WEA 2101CS COMSEC 315FTD 340BMS ADC TA SPVR______

RATUZYUW RUCVAAA1335 1282251-UUUU--RUCIBEA.
ZNR UUUUU
R 082215Z MAY 89
FM 1CEVG BARKSDALE AFB LA//ST//
TO RUCIBEA/97BMW EAKER AFB AR//CC/DO//
RUCUAAA/HQ SAC OFFUTT AFB NE//DO//
AIG 10403//CC/DO//
INFO RUCUAAA/HQ SAC OFFUTT AFB NE//DOT/DONP/IGX/CG/CK//
ZEN 8AF BARKSDALE AFB LA//DO/DOOK/DOT/RF//
ZEN 2BMW BARKSDALE AFB LA//CC/DO//
RUEAUSA/HGB WASHINGTON DC//XOOTS//
BT
UNCLAS
QQQQ
SUBJ:  RESULTS OF 1CEVG EVALUATION COMPLETED ON 6 MAY 89
1.  UNIT CHECKED:  97 BOMBARDMENT WING, EAKER AFB, AR
A.  OVERALL UNIT RATING                          SATISFACTORY
2.  AIRCREW PERFORMANCE                          SATISFACTORY
A.  INFLIGHT QL-1 QL-2 QL-3 TOTAL
(1) B-52 34 2 6 42 UNSATISFACTORY
(2) KC-135 24 1 0 25 OUTSTANDING
(3) COMBINED 58 3 6 67 MARGINAL


PAGE 02 RUCVAAA1335 UNCLAS
B.  GROUND AVTIVITY
(1)  EMERGENCY PROCEDURE EXAMS
(A) B-52 159 0 0 159 OUTSTANDING
(B) KC-135 73 0 0 73 OUTSTANDING
(2) ATD (B-52) 9 0 0 9 OUTSTANDING
(3) COMBINED 241 0 0 241 OUTSTANDING
C.  STANDARDIZATION PROGRAM                      SATISFACTORY
D.  TRAINING PROGRAM                             SATISFACTORY
3.  THE 97BMW HAS A COMPREHENSIVE TACTICS PROGRAM THAT IS PROVIDING
INNOVATIVE AND REALISTIC TRAINING.  CONTINUATION TRAINING AND WST
UTILIZATION RATES WERE STRENGTHS.  DEGRADED BOMBING SYSTEM OPERATION
WAS A WEAKNESS WHICH CONTRIBUTED TO THE BOMBER'S UNSATISFACTORY
FLIGHT RATING.

BT
#1335  NNNN
```

Left: Base inspection paperwork

Below: A ghostly shell

An Alert Facility bathroom

Retired Delta MD-80/MD-90 on the Christmas Tree (Alert Pad)

Building 1225 and its swimming pool

What once was an everyday sight …

Building 92, overgrown

Valve in a water refinement station

"Change is an opportunity"

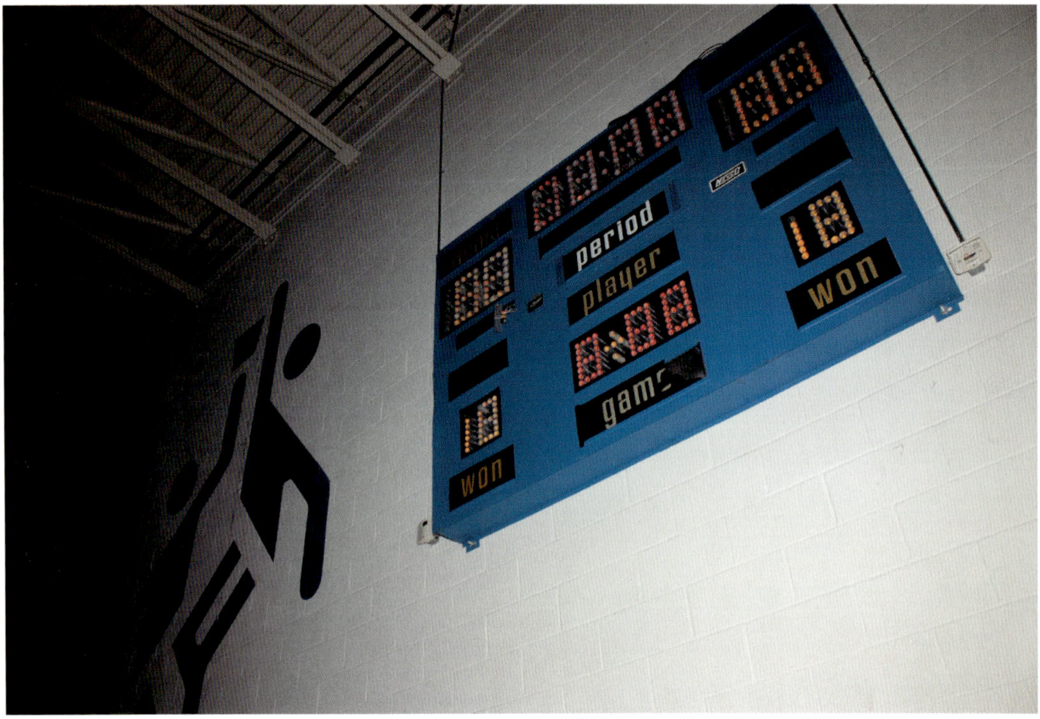

The scoreboard in the large gym of the YMCA

The small gym of the YMCA

9

BLYTHEVILLE AND THE COLD WAR

On December 20, 1972, the third day of Operation Linebacker II came to a close with a loss to the United States Air Force and Blytheville Air Force Base. Two bombers with Blytheville airmen were shot down during the heavy bombing mission over the capital of Vietnam, Hanoi. Callsign Olive 01, with Lieutenant Colonel Keith Heggen aboard, went down. Callsign Tan 03 went down as well. Of the seven Blytheville crewmembers aboard, only one survived and became a prisoner of war for a year. He was then repatriated in March of 1973.

It was a known fact that the G models did not have advanced systems of radar technology like the D models had. The Vietnamese had used this fact to their advantage, As the bombers had turned away from their targets, it was discovered there was a pocket that the land-to-air missiles could lock on to. The G models could not defend themselves with radar-jamming facing the back of the aircraft. Though the Vietnamese had to hand crank their launchers to line up a shot, G models were their main focus.

The United States caught on to this problem fast, and immediately commanded crews to start banking their bombers after dropping their payloads, thus decreasing the chance of being shot down. The local military and government had collected pieces of the wreckage of a bomber from Linebacker II and displayed it in the city as a memorial to commemorate the "overcoming of western imperialism." Today that memorial still stands outside a "victory museum" in Hanoi.

There is currently a memorial dedicated to those of Blytheville Air Force Base that were lost during Operation Linebacker II. It stands along Memorial Drive in front of the former base hospital. It is routinely maintained. The memorial consists of a concrete and polished granite base. A cast iron plate was built into the face that explains the importance of the memorial and dedicates it to those lost. At the bottom are photos of the crewmembers. Atop of the base is a large metal sculpture of a B-52.

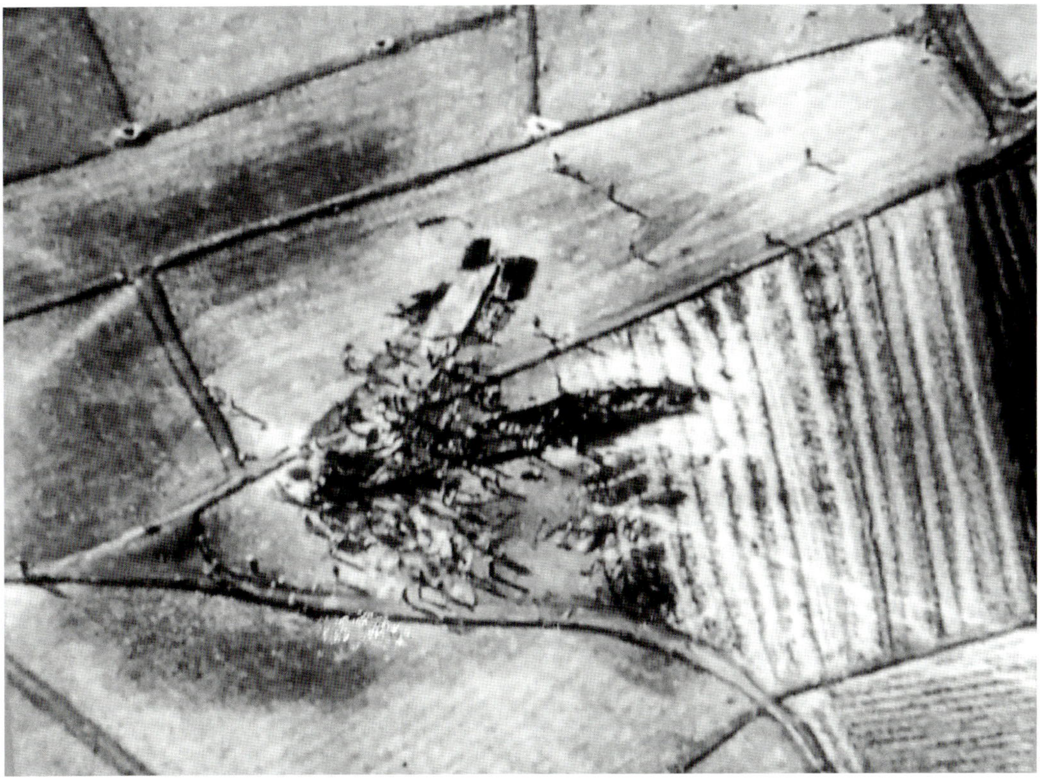

Above: Linebacker II crash near Hanoi

Right: Linebacker II memorial in front of the hospital

The sculpture is securely mounted through the base and has to be lifted by a crane to move.

During the Cold War, the Strategic Air Command oversaw 250,000 air men. Bombers were deployed to as many as fifty countries during the entire span of the war. Strategic Air Command also oversaw all nuclear weapons, such as the LGM-25C Titan II. There were over fifteen Titan II silos in Arkansas, mostly based around "the Rock." Multiple events occurred in Arkansas alone, the most well-known being the Damascus explosion of 1980. Fifteen years earlier, a far deadlier and grimmer event happened. In 1965, while performing maintenance on a silo, just eleven miles north of Searcy, a fire broke out. This was known as the Titan II Silo 373-4 tragedy. Fifty-three workers had died in the fire.

In 1959, the S.A.C. documented a study for "political" reasons that was declassified in 2015. At over 800 pages long, it described a list of targets the United States had selected for either fully atomic/nuclear bombing, or less lethal bombing. The reasoning for the study was to "differentiate countries from the Soviet Union." During this time, the S.A.C. had over 100 atomic weapons that they would deploy onto Soviet targets in a thirty-day period if a situation were to ever arise. This all was part of the Emergency War Plan 1-49. On average, fifteen bombers were stationed at the base at a time. The same goes for the tankers.

Blytheville's main unit was the 97th Bombardment Wing, tasked with combat operations of the B-52 Stratofortress. This wing had its own support elements such as the 97th Air Refueling Squadron, and the 97th Organizational Maintenance Squadron, tasked with repairing aircraft. The 97th Bombardment Wing was one of the highest scoring wings in the Air Force's ORI program. The 97th Bombardment Wing was a four-time winner of the Air Force's Outstanding Unit Award. The unit had also at one point won the Fairchild Trophy. This trophy was presented to outstanding bombing units.

Blytheville's units won the title of "Best Armory" in 1983 and the Omaha Trophy (a prestigious award given to the S.A.C. 's "best wing").

In the last years of the Cold War, through the years leading up to and through the Persian Gulf War, Blytheville had passed many Air Force inspections with unheard of scores. The 97th Bombardment Wing scored the highest "Probability of Damage" in S.A.C. history with a score of .998 in 1989.

Though not part of Blytheville history, during World War II, the 97th Bombardment Wing had earned two Distinguished Unit Citations from missions during said war.

10

THE LOSS OF HULK 46

One story that is shrouded in mystery involving Blytheville is the loss of a United States aircraft known as HULK 46. The B-52 Stratofortress (Serial Number 59-2593) was involved in the Persian Gulf War. Very early in the morning on February 3, 1991, after departing from the U.S. base in Diego Garcia, the aircraft mysteriously went M.I.A. The aircraft had plunged into the Indian Ocean, fifty miles north of Diego Garcia.

The crew were assigned to the 97th Bombardment Wing of Blytheville. They were on temporary duty assignment. Of the six to man the bomber, only three had survived. One was never recovered. The three that did survive were said to smell profusely like jet fuel.

The bomber was never fully recovered. Full details of the crash are still unknown as the documents are still classified. Though some blame the pilot, some the electronics, and some blame other circumstances. Today, a nonprofit organization is working to construct a memorial in dedication of the lost. It will be built on the grounds of the base hospital in Blytheville next to the Linebacker II memorial.

The crew of the doomed HULK 46

11

BASE CLOSURE

In order to understand why Eaker Air Force Base closed, one has to dive into foreign, political, and socioeconomic issues of the late 1980s and early 1990s. The Cold War had come to an end. Communism had shriveled in the world. The Iron Curtain was torn down. Mr. Gorbachev tore down that wall. And the United States was about to enter war with Saddam Hussein.

The United States no longer needed bombers and fuel-tankers to be on 24/7 alert. The Strategic Air Command had reached the end of the road. There was no need for the Global Shield. Americans did not have to fear every day of an imminent Soviet nuclear attack.

In the years leading up to the reunification of Germany, the U.S. government sought out to begin a process that would eventually cause many bases like Eaker to be closed. In the late 1980s, the government, under congress, had begun inspections on Air Force bases. This would determine if the base could go on operating in the future, or if it was deemed unnecessary to continue service. The process is called B.R.A.C.

Under the Federal Property and Administrative Services Act of 1949, the United States government is obligated to consider utilization, procurement, and disposal of government property. After any major war, surplus equipment and property is sold to the general public and agencies. Property is disposed of and the government cleans up after itself.

B.R.A.C. action specifically caters to closures and revitalization of U.S. bases. From the late 1980s until 1990, Eaker Air Force Base was on the top of the list. In December of 1992, the base officially closed. The Air Force packed up and left, leaving Little Rock as Arkansas' only active base.

In 1985, a bill was signed to regulate federal spending. It is known as The Balanced Budget and Emergency Deficit Control Act of 1985. In short, this bill was created

This way please …

to balance the federal budget. Specific requirements were made for government entities to meet, and if they did not meet those requirements, budgets would be cut.

Hangars on the base were built too large for modern aircraft. Eaker Air Force Base was also only a single mission base, and that single mission was to launch and receive G model variants of the B-52. Blytheville was also a single wing base. But when the 1990s rolled around, U.S. military spending decreased as the Cold War came to an end. The U.S. was under provisions of the START I treaty with the U.S.S.R.

This treaty was an agreement between both countries to reduce and limit their nuclear powers and technology. This included lowering the numbers of their ICBMs, submarine-launched ballistic missiles, bombers, and warheads. Though this treaty expired in 2009, it was quickly replaced by a new treaty, New Start, signed by President Barack Obama in April of 2010. Due to this treaty, over 500 B-52s were sent to Arizona to be scrapped at A.M.A.R.C

The effect of the closure on the neighboring towns of Gosnell and Blytheville were tremendous. Gosnell reported losing over half its students. Thousands of jobs were lost. The local economy tanked and unemployment skyrocketed. In 1990, Blytheville's population was 23,443. Today it is 14,011. Granted, today the area has stayed well-populated due to industrial jobs, but Blytheville's unemployment rate is four percent higher than the national average.

The new enlisted dorms

On the November 12, 1992, the last B-52, named "Memphis Belle III," left Eaker Air Force Base. This marked the end of an era with a sorrowful goodbye. The entire event was broadcasted by KAIT 8 and Channel 13 News.

In 1984, an investigation of cleanup began under the Defense Environmental Restoration Program on the base and discovered over thirty major environmental risk sites on the base including former landfills, waste disposals, and many underground storage tanks. The largest worry with environmental risks were petroleum hydrocarbons, PFAS, and PFOA. These dangerous materials were primarily found in firefighting materials, especially AFFF (aqueous film-forming foam). The report, when finished in 1985, was 198 pages long. It is easily accessible online.

The D.E.R.P. report culminated in a Draft Environmental Impact Statement on January 29, 1990, when the Secretary of Defense announced closure of Eaker Air Force Base. In November of 1992, a Final Environmental Impact Statement (also easily accessible online) was released. This F.E.I.S. (over 600 pages long) recorded everything from sound pollution, to reuse of sectors of the base, to wildlife being affected before and after closure.

In 1996, the U.S.A.F. began cleanup on the base under a Base Realignment Plan, which lasted until 2015. Many RFIs, CMSs, SEBSs, and FOSTs were filed and revised throughout that time. The EPA, DOD, and ADEQ spent over thirty-five million dollars in cleanup, and plan to spend another six million to be finished by 2050.

It wouldn't be until 1999 that the base saw official use again, this time under the control of the Arkansas Aeroplex. While the apron and alert pad went under the Aeroplex's control, the rest of the base, such as the Westminster Village, went under control of numerous private and public entities. Since then, the base has fallen into a sad state of repair beyond many official entities' control.

12

LIFE AFTER THE BOMBERS

Since Eaker Air Force Base went under B.R.A.C. action, it has sat mostly dormant. Businesses have come and go, but the wear and tear of Mother Nature and Father time have taken their toll on many buildings on base. The worst building on base is the hospital. Though it may have been locked and boarded up (with half inch steel plates over all the glass), it stands in the worst condition.

Holes in the roof create entryways for birds and rain. Mold and asbestos float through the air like dust that just got kicked up. Tiling soaked in stagnant water sloshes under your feet, and anything that could be rusted is rusted. It is very possible the paint peeling on the walls is lead-based.

The hospital has been tightly sealed up due to the high amount of asbestos flying around in the air and the safety concerns. The hospital is also a very large building in terms of square footage, so it is very possible to get lost inside the building without a map.

The headquarters of the 97th Bombardment Wing is in terrible condition as well. It has the exact same problems as the hospital, though both buildings trade off on extremities. The building has water standing at one-foot deep, and the rafters of the building in certain rooms have collapsed so far that they touch the ground. This happens to be isolated to the center of the building. While it may be the most accessible area of the building, it is extremely difficult to navigate through and out of that area, due to water above your feet, the floor falling out from under you, the risk of tripping and being cut open by smashed glass, or rusted metal.

The accounting and financing building has a large and open floor plan. It is a peculiarly shaped building, like the rest of the buildings on the base. Currently, the wet carpet has molded repeatedly. The walls have been smashed through, possibly due to delinquents "having fun." All the glass has been shattered.

The majority of buildings have suffered the same fate, from an extreme case of having to be boarded up like a top-secret quarantine, to simply being an old tool

A hallway inside the YMCA

The Accounting and Finance building

shed that never got used. Certain buildings are worth saving. The theater is one of the best-preserved buildings on the base. The YMCA building is also a very well-preserved building, despite the amount of graffiti it has collected in just one year.

Many buildings are gone. And will continue to disappear. Whether it be by the hand of the elements, or by deconstruction due to safety issues.

Despite the poor condition of numerous buildings around the base, Eaker Air Force Base is home to the only publicly accessible Alert Facility in the world. Said facility is also the only one with its swimming pool still intact. Eaker Air Force Base is the only S.A.C.-era installation with an intact "family planning" center and operational Pulsar gates.

The base isn't entirely abandoned though. Since 1991, the housing has been used as "Westminster Village." The chapel has been in use as well. The preschool and the Family Services buildings are still in use. The bowling alley still operates, though it isn't the hottest spot in the area. The firing range and golf course is still in use to this day as well.

The main portion of the base being the tarmac, hangars, fire department, and control tower are still in use today as the Arkansas Aeroplex. The former base is now also home to Aviation Repair Technologies. A.R.T. is a FAA and EASA-certified industry-leading company tasked with the maintenance, storage, and salvaging of aircraft in the United States.

Since 2020, A.R.T. and the Arkansas Aeroplex have been tasked with the storage and salvage operations of many MD-88s and MD-90s retired by Delta Airlines.

Right: The entrance to the E.R. at the hospital

Below: A computer left behind at a water refinement station

Inside the 97th BMW building

Housing

The theater

The N.C.O. Club kitchen

Left: Inside the enlisted dorms

Below: The Strato-Club

13

THE FUTURE AND THE NATIONAL COLD WAR CENTER

Due to the local economy suffering after Eaker AFB was "B.R.A.C.'d," multiple buildings on the base were put up for sale, but never put to use properly. Owners had big ambitions to renovate and repurpose the old buildings, but either plan never took off or funding ran out. This led to the current dilapidated state of some buildings.

Though it is currently in a rough shape as an Air Force Base, it doesn't have to be that way. Currently, there is a restoration program working to rebuild and reuse buildings that haven't been claimed back by nature to sink into the farmland from which it grew.

The program consists of multiple contractors working to bring buildings that are far beyond repair down and save buildings that can be saved before it's too late. This has been an ongoing project for over a year. On January 23, 2022, it was announced that the former dorms would be demolished. On January 1, 2022, the former base bank had been torn down. On February 21, 2022, the former N.C.O. Club was demolished.

The base's former theater is to be saved, as well as the former "YMCA." In 2021, the Mississippi county had granted the National Cold War Center and the Arkansas Aeroplex $50,000 to restore the theater. On January 11, during Agile Combat Employment training exercises performed by the U.S. Air Force at Eaker Air Force Base, work began on the restoration process of Building 1225. Doors and numerous truckloads of metal were being hauled off the alert pad

In 2020, Arkansas senators proposed a bill to designate the museum in Blytheville as the National Cold War Center. Senator Boozman is quoted saying:

Building 1225, March 2022

> The Blytheville Air Force Base exhibition is dedicated to sharing the stories and educating the public about the community's role in our national security. I'm proud to honor the accomplishments of the men and women who served at Eaker Air Force Base by recognizing the museum as the National Cold War Center so we can pay tribute to their contributions to our defense.

On January 31, 2022, the Arkansas Aeroplex officially announced that work had started on restoration of Building 1225. Roof repairs began on February 19, 2022. Electrical work and flood damage followed soon after. Five feet of water was pumped out of the basement of the building. The National Cold War Center is planned to be the largest collection of history and information on the decades that made up the war, with everything from a static display of a B-52 Stratofortress to letters from soldiers to their families overseas.

Building 1225 will be added to the collection of buildings as part of the future National Cold War Center. It is planned to be its own exhibit within the system of buildings. The current BAFB Exhibit is housed in the former B-52 crew briefing building and will continue to be an exhibit.

The National Cold War Center will be an entirely brand-new building itself. It will be designed to be the shape of a B-52 Stratofortress. Building 1225 is currently registered on the National Register of Historic Places and is quoted as being the "crown jewel of the National Cold War Center campus." Though Phase Two of the project is underway (as of June 2022), there have been no announcements of when the museum will officially open.

N.C.W.C. Board of Directors, breaking ground, March 2022

Two Barksdale B52s taxiing in, January 2022

Just a skeleton

Target in the Personnel Division

Target in the Personnel Division

Dummy grenade on the floor

Longing for the day to see Alerts be performed again…

Valkyrie mural painted on a wall

Almost like they just left for the night and never came back

Time sits still here …

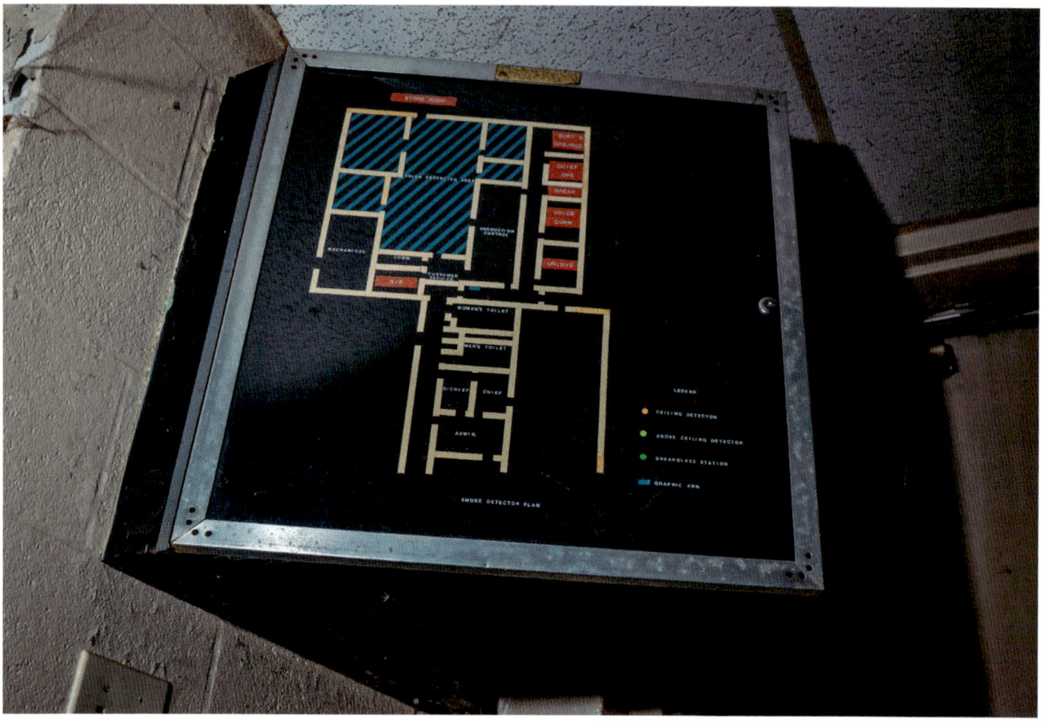
STORE ROOM
CHIEF OPS
BREAK
VOICE COMM
PRODUCTION CONTROL
MECHANICAL
COMM
CUSTOMER SERVICE
S/E
UNISYS
WOMEN'S TOILET
MEN'S TOILET
D/CHIEF
CHIEF
ADMIN.
LEGEND
CEILING DETECTOR
ABOVE CEILING DETECTOR
BREAKGLASS STATION
GRAPHIC ANN
SMOKE DETECTOR PLAN

Welcome home

Clockwise from right:

A light on the back of a hangar

WW2 tower

The control tower, 2022

WW2 hangar

The failed expansion of the Westminster Village

View of Building 1225 from the sallyport at sunset

Munitions storage

Watch tower near munitions storage
at sunset

Control house at the silos

The A.A.F.E.S. Exchange Hall post-cleanup, 2022

Blytheville Air Force Base fire rig, pre-1988

Front gate

Security Police

97th Civil Engineering Squadron motorpool

Some downtime with fellow airmen

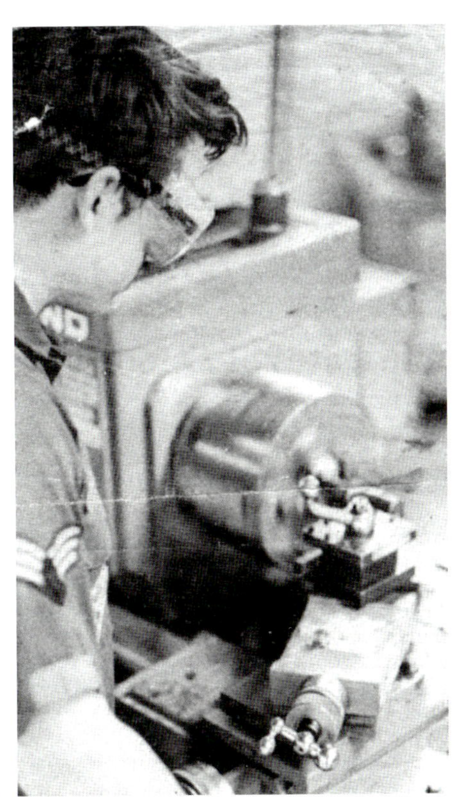

Machining new parts

Engine swap, done the USAF way

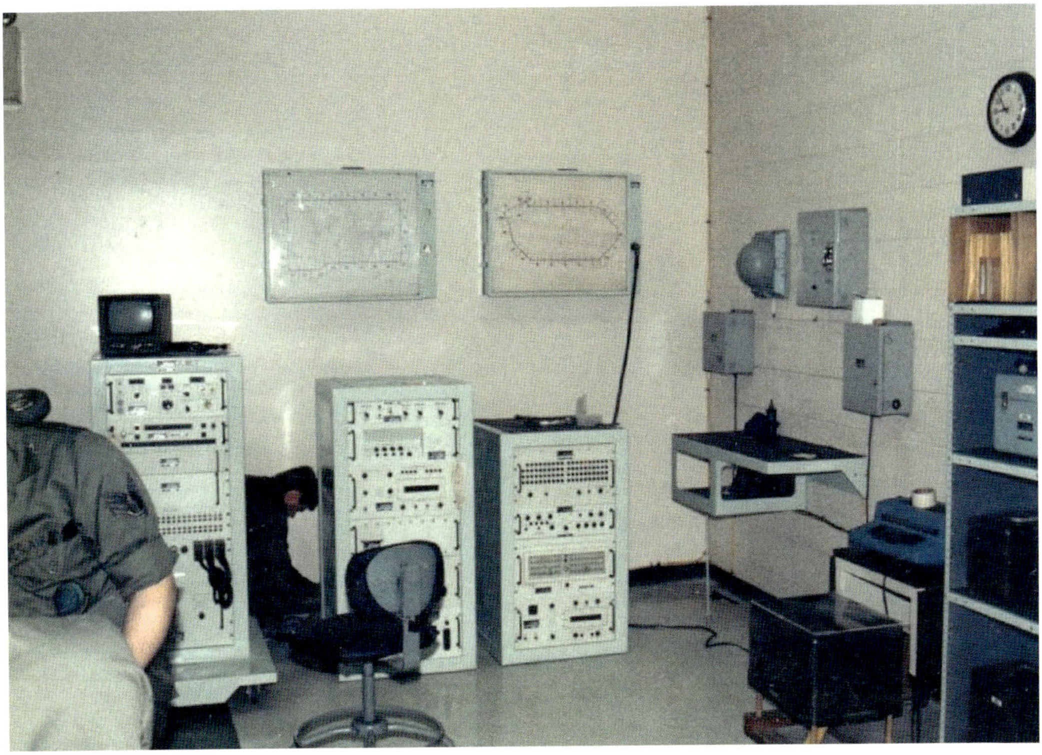

A lot of computing power

Take care of your equipment and it will take care of you

All lined up and ready

Loading ordinances into a B-52

Tail #2599 and her crew

Above: The last S.A.C. DC-3/C-47 at Blytheville AFB

Right: Aerial/Satellite, unknown date

Left: Engine maintenance

Below: KC-135 #61-0226

97th SPS

Party at the Strato-Club

T.A.C. Era Blytheville Bomber (B57)

In the old law enforcement building

The First National Bank, 2021 (before demolition)

AUTHOR'S NOTES

While writing this, the National Cold War Center is still in the construction phase (February 2023). By the time one reads this, the museum may already be completed and open to the public.

Eaker Air Force Base as a whole is a mix of federal and private properties. I do not encourage nor condone any others to openly explore the base without any form of permission. Trespassing especially on the flight pad is a felony and can cost upwards of $10,000 in fines or a very lengthy jail time.

This book was made possible with help from my supportive family, Technical Sergeant Robert Charles, the NCWC, the Mississippi County Museum in Osceola, the Delta Gateway Museum, the Jacksonville Museum of Military History, the 97th Air Mobility Wing, as well as my preacher, Leon, and his wife.

PHOTO CREDITS

Historical photos courtesy of The National Cold War Center, the 97th Air Mobility Wing of Altus AFB, and the Wings of Honor Museum in Walnut Ridge, Arkansas.

Extra photos are courtesy of Aubrey Hansen.

The Patricia Kenworth photo is courtesy of Texas Women's University.

The W.A.S.P. group photo is courtesy of Encyclopedia Britannica.

The photo of B-52 (tail number 61-0023) photo is courtesy of the USAF.

The 61-0023 crew photo is courtesy of Boeing.

The Ira Eaker photo is listed under Public Domain.

The photo of 61-023 and its crew is courtesy of Boeing.

BIBLIOGRAPHY

"Boeing KC-46 Pegasus Tanker" - Aeroweb

"SALT Treaties" - Encyclopedia.com

"Strategic Arms Reduction Treaty of 1991" - National Parks Service

"KC-135 Stratotanker" - Nuclear Resources

"Eaker Air Force Base" - Military History Fandom

"Historical Snapshot: B-52 Stratofortress" - Boeing

"Historical Snapshot: KC135 Stratotanker" - Boeing

"S.1771 - National Cold War Center Act of 2021" - Congress.gov

 HULK46 - About

"Strategic Air Command" - Britannica

"Bill Designating National Cold War Center in Blytheville Introduced in Senate" -
    Boozeman.senate.gov

"General Ira C. Eaker" - USAF official website

"Former Eaker AFB (BRAC 1991)" - USAF Civil Engineer Center

 nationalcoldwarcenter.com/

"Female WWII Pilots: The Original Fly Girls" - NPR

"History of Eaker AFB 1942-1988" - NCWC

"Timeline of Blytheville" - NCWC

"B-52G And H Assignments, 1958-1994" - NCWC